THE GIFT

The Wisdom

Of

Nefertiti

As

I AM

Francis E. Revels-Bey

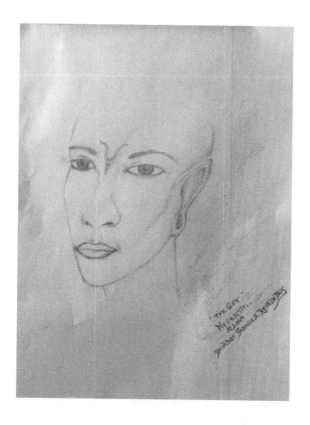

The is a "Meditative Drawing of Beloved Nefertiti" by the author Francis E. Revels-Bey on 2/15-16/2019. He asked his wonderful Sister Vernell to help him choose amongst 8 drawings and she chose number 8 of 8. Brother Francis & Sister Vernell are very happy with her choice as it "feels right". It was rendered with a No. 2 pencil to help maintain her gentle beauty and inner strength that shines through as well.

THE GIFT - The Wisdom Of Nefertiti As I AM
Copyright © 2019 - Francis E. Revels-Bey
All rights reserved.

First Edition.
Printed in the United States of America

ISBN: 9781731060761

Table of Contents

Dedication

I, Brother Francis E. Revels-Bey, am so grateful that Nefertiti is communicating this special channeled work through me so that there is a companion text equal to Ahkenaten's, as she is the twin solar flame to Our Beloved Ahkenaten. This channeled message reveals to the reader the mutual understanding that they had for each other through the Celestial connection that brought them together that infinitely expresses itself across the vast and infinite galactic domain. As Amenaten, I remembered the whisperings going on behind their backs from the Amun priesthood who were so upset that they "came" to anoint the people - royalty and non-royalty alike with their own connection to their divine selves. As Nefertiti said *"They did everything they could to make us look like we were against each other, but we never did succumb to their plots because we are one. These kinds of antics still go on into modern times. So never allow yourself to forget who you truly are beloveds."*

Beloved Nefertiti is a true master like Beloved Ahkenaten and they both have a bond that can never be broken. They both only place a portion of themselves in all of us who have been their initiates so that we can go forward with the various degrees of their teachings through our eternal remembrances of them.

Beloved Nefertiti, you came as a Gift and thus this material is penned "THE GIFT - The Wisdom Of Nefertiti As I AM".

Yes, I AM forever grateful to have become one of many chosen to channel this MA-terial for you.

A Spiritual Transmission from
The Divine Conscious Self

Blessings to All Divine Ones who are aware of their remembrances coming forward in their respective lifetimes from moment to moment. Every moment is coming in successive waves through The Presence of the Divine Mother. Allow yourselves to remain present so that you, too, can begin to remember all that is not only necessary for your evolution, but for your return back into the Infinite Celestial Divine Source forever known as The Great Central Sun.

As Amenaten, I write this from my Divine Conscious Self as a living example so that many others can begin to remember their own divinity as the New Earth is unfolding on behalf of the collective humanity as they reawaken as Divine I AM Beings. Be aware of the infinite possibilities referred to as time-lines as these are overflowing with numerous frequencies that we can all tap into at the right times. We are all here to advance ourselves so that we are free of the 3D Matrix. All that we see in the 3D

Matrix is illusionary and that is why the miscreated ego can get stuck within it and cause us to believe that this is where everything truly is when that is not true.

Raise your personal frequency and you will begin to have less contact with the lower frequencies and you shall be drawn to "beings, energies, and/or places" that harmonize with your internal world. It is your internal world where you truly are alive and well. Do not hold on to each other so tightly as you can cause each other to miss out on new and exciting adventures while striving to advance yourselves. Be sure to spend a healthy amount of quiet time in Silence as this helps you recharge and stay aligned and attuned to higher frequencies that are correct for you.

There are so many of us now with our divine natures already being activated again in this life time and thus, it is highly important that we all continue to expand our awareness, delve into our unique remembrances and call upon our Angelic Soul Essences while implementing our Divine Solar and

Galactic fields within our auric fields. There is a great deal of cleansing that must continue to happen so you can gain access to the higher frequencies beyond your physical world. There are new divine technologies as templates being created and many more already beyond this veil just right for all of you. You must continue to reach outward and connect with your divine spiritual tribes as you reach deep inside yourself as well. No one is ever left behind unless it is their choice. One of us and many of us shall pull others into higher folds of energy due to the continuous opening of our higher petals of light.

All of these earthly events and sporadic happenings that we see in the 3D matrix are present to spur many of us forward and will cause many of us to remember to leave clear footsteps for others to discover and those who are ready to move out of it. There are many events that will trigger your deeper desires to move in harmonic step with the currents of ascension. Take care of yourselves for it can be easy and yet you might find yourself moving too quickly without being centered. There are many distractions around you that seem to fall into your path. This is why spending time in the silent chamber within you is essential to your well-being. Learn to choose your currents to ride forward and not against so that you can achieve all that you truly desire.

Last, remember that you are not becoming a divine conscious self. No, you are already that and more. While you are diligently working to return to the highest frequencies within The Great Central Sun, remember that you have the many seeds of GCS within you so you can demonstrate lots of it here in whatever dimension you find yourself in as it is not going to take another million years or even 5,000 years for it can literally happen in minutes because of who you truly are...One with The Infinite Divine Celestial Source.

One of many Keys is Remembrance !

The Author's Remembrance of Nefertiti
as Amenaten

Greetings and welcome to this divine treat from Nefertiti as I am Beloved Amenaten and this is my channeled memory and salubrious opportunity to present Nefertiti's wisdom to all of you. When, Beloved Master Teacher Ahkenaten had his divine temples built for his technologies involving ascension, his beautiful and equally wise partner, Master Nefertiti was always present and clearly instructing all of us. There were many times that their energy was so strong while teaching us that their bodies would move from the physical carbon body into crystalline light.

I deeply remember being directly instructed and initiated through the Path of The Cobra and they simultaneously shape shifted from their physical forms into the Living Cobras of Light before my eyes. Also, they were the Orbs of Divinity hovering above the pyramids as well. There were many moments within their Ascension Chambers where all of us, either laid on the floor of the temple or seated on the ascension seats, were transported by way of soul traveling into the heart of the temples within The Great Central Sun. Nefertiti could freely communicate with all of us telepathically, as well as, doing that often with Ahkenaten.

Not once have I ever witnessed Beloved Nefertiti abuse her power or authority as she was always centered on being supportive to Ahkenaten and she made extra sure that he was respected after his reign. Eventually, she became well sought after for all of her wisdom and she never failed to share it. Beloved Nefertiti had foreseen how there was so much that had to be done and exactly how all of us had to be prepared when the priesthood began to encircle them with all of their negative assumptions and mass anger, but Nefertiti was an adept warrior of the light and along with Ahkenaten moved us out of harm's way. She is a woman with great power who is truly an Ascension Master and Blessing to All of Us. Get ready to receive....*THE GIFT - The Wisdom of Nefertiti As I AM through the eyes of Beloved Amenaten.*

Introduction by Beloved I AM Nefertiti

"Beloveds, ***I AM Nefertiti*** *~* ***The Beloved Gift &*** ***Pillar of The Blue Flame*** *and I have come in this moment to share this Gift of Oneness as THE CELESTIAL ~SOLAR PRESENCE OF THE I AM. What is now happening is that you are coming back to yourself...Yes, it is The Gathering of All of Your Soul Elements coming to you for you are the one who called yourself into being through the Primary Infinite and Divine Source Code of One. I represent the God Conscious Self that is inherent in every being. You, as humanity, are at the precipice of a new day despite what you really see before your eyes. As changes occur in the external you see it fueled by fear and fear is the lack of love_for each other. We are asking that as you remember your divinity that you come forward and share it by allowing yourself to be more of the light that you have always been. There are many souls coming forward that really do remember The I AM Presence that is of the expression of The Divine Mother-Father God. This Divine Mother Energy carries the Blue Ray and All Other*

Rays as The Blue Flame and is very healing as it creates harmonic peace and wholeness. Meditate daily and your light frequencies get clearer in due time. Ahkenaten and I came into this world as Twin Flame Souls. The higher frequencies of my Celestial Mission with Beloved Ahkenaten goes beyond the appearance of being twin flames, as well as, beyond and through The Petals Of Light (Heart Chakra) as Our God Conscious Self is The Living Soul as a Divine Nature Activated and now We are One.

THE GIFT is Our Awareness and Remembrance of Being One through our organic relationship as a Divine Aegis within The Great Central Sun. This channeled MATER-I-AL is being offered to you through Amenaten's remembrance. There are time-lines carrying higher frequencies and these shall be coming into being as you all begin to transcend. Understand that the souls who are still on the playground in the 3D Matrix are there because they choose to be there. Symbolically, understand the parts of the word "Material" as Ma, Mate, Mater, Ter, I and Al as Mother - Mate-Mother-Three-I - The...the message is hidden as "The Mate to The Mother is I AM". So when we understand that the Divine Father comes into Absolute Harmony with the Divine Mother everything, everyone and every element shall continue to transcend as One."

1

The Gift of Oneness

My Beloved Ahkenaten and I in essence "walked into" these bodies where we delivered the teachings to all who were ready. We prepared many of you for these moments of ascension and transcendence through many moments of silence so that you could recognize that you are the absolute gateway - the open door to go back into the celestial realms. We both taught the Left Eye and Right Eye of Horus so that you can begin to remember the dance between the two shall eventually become one. The external dance shows up as feminine and masculine forms of beings, but the true dance is the presence within personified by the double cobras. You must override your miscreated self - your ego for it stands between you being separated or being connected to your divine celestial self.

We taught you how to go within and I desire to give you another method later that primes your well-being and swiftly opens all of the Petals of Light. It's not about envisioning yourself as a light force...it is about KNOWING that YOU ARE A LIGHT FORCE and it is not about whether or not if anyone can see your light because it is about REMEMBERING THAT YOU ARE OF THE LIGHT. As you begin to remember that you are light, then grow in your awareness and remembrance that within the body's energy field you are displaying a field of energy that emits even frequencies of light which can freely communicate throughout the multi-universe of infinite higher realms of consciousness. Many of you are beginning to remember that there are different time-lines around you and these time-lines carry different frequencies within them. These time-lines are overflowing with gemstone keys connected to activating one's ability, capacity and skill to communicate with the celestial realms so that you can return from whence you came. Above all else remember that you carry within yourself infinite frequencies flowing from your Higher-Self / Soul / Celestial Being.

We taught all of you to realize that your highest goal is to become one with All of the Sources of

Divinity. The use of Meditation and Invocational Prayers are to help you trigger your rich connection to the Divine Source of All That Is and Evermore Shall Be. Beloveds kindly honor yourselves in every moment for in every moment you are truly divine. We are all given many opportunities to achieve this process and to allow ourselves to learn all that we can, and can remember. No matter where you find yourself, you can always give yourself permission to receive this blessing.

As you begin to encounter these opportunities there will always be some kind of challenge that appears to be beyond your level of understanding, but they are really not. Sometimes you forget that you created some of them while others did their part in creating these obstacles and your environment presented others. If you fail to realize this, then everything can appear to you as difficult. This happens because you are becoming more entrapped in the illusions around you as they appear real to you and real to the collective minds. Most of the time the collective minds come to agree that these illusions are now the reality because they appear to be quite comfortable and are therefore easy to achieve and should be admired. Nonetheless, the journey is real for everyone. You will find yourself questioning everything that you do and this sets up confusion within yourself, now you feel lost or devalued. If you allow the emotional part of you to come into play, then you start to worry and doubt yourself when you should not do so.

You must begin to look within for your answers. Come back to yourself and embrace yourself. Let me say that again: *Come back to yourself and Embrace yourself.* This is essential to your well-being. Embrace your divinity for that is your original self. Next, balance your emotional and your mental parts of yourself as these are tools that help you discern your environment. Do not over react or over act....in other words, stop responding to everything that you encounter along your path. There are just somethings you need not pay attention to but you just be aware of its presence. Discern its value and if it has none then do not respond. We all share one precious commodity and that is ENERGY. We never deplete it as it only changes form or takes on different forms in your environment.

We must all embrace the fact that we share in the use of energy which is used all of the time no matter where you are or what you are doing with it. Energy takes on the form in your environment of five elements which are: Fire, Air, Water, Earth and Ether. Since we are also Energy Beings we are processing these elements as well but on higher levels. These elements are fueled by interaction with each other, other higher forces and especially with the waves of energy coming from the Sun and the Great Central Sun which is why you feel good when you receive sun rays by sitting within the rays while outside your dwellings or seated before a window to receive them when inside your dwellings. We utilize the sun to revitalize, purify and raise our energy levels deep within us.

The whole idea of drawing on the solar, lunar and other planetary system energies is to harness it so that when you are out and away from its presence you have the source in you to draw on and use these to create expansion, etc., when needed. Once you attain oneness and can maintain the connection, then you are on your way back to being resourceful and at One with All.

2

The Gathering

Beloveds, I have previously mentioned that we all share a common commodity called Energy. We can excel on our own as an individual seeking the infinite light of divinity. But, there are moments when you can reach that same destiny by coming together with like-minded souls, souls who share the same interests, knowledge, wisdom and understanding. There will be other souls who already have a key or keys you may not possess or not yet mastered. So it is important to develop gatherings so that you can educate and assist each other's ascension. Some gatherings are still taking place quietly and that is to protect certain keys so they are not abused or misused and that's because they carry a very high frequency. However, more Souls like yourselves carry high internal electromagnetic frequencies that draw these tools to yourselves anyway simply because you are ready for them.

What my Beloved Ahkenaten and I love so dearly is that many of you are recognizing each other through deeper levels of personal and group meditations, invocational prayer circles, through the dream world and soul travelings. Your levels of awareness are forever increasing and you are having higher levels of remembrance.

But, what about those of you who just desire to do the gathering with higher beings such as angelic forces, elementals in nature or even your own master cells from within you. Here is a transformational tool that can help you do that. It is an initiatory tool so keep in mind that if you do it daily and consistently you will see yourself in the flow and feel the presence of the beings. Then you will have established an active "working relationship" with them. This method is very much like meditation but mostly of a "call and response" kind of meditation as it involves the use one of the following - or you may use more than one "Key":

Breath, Vocal Sound /Your Intentions

Ancestors, Ancestral Guide(s), Deity

Universal and / or Personal Symbol

Tuning Forks

Crystal Bowls

Crystals / Gemstones

Candle(s) / Incense

The second precious commodity is BREATH and so I am going to teach you how to apply this infinite key so that you can experience the sensation and feeling when applying it to ascertain a direct connection and then maintain that connection. Now, since I am bringing my teaching into your surroundings, I have chosen for you to establish a direct and continuous connection with a TREE. The tree you seek may be on your living premises or down the road or in what you call a park. This will not be a one day experience, because when the connection is made you will continue to repeat the method for at lease what is referred to as two weeks in your time-line. But, you will quickly learn that the Tree is "Calling Out" to You ! That is correct. The tree is already consciously aware of your presence within its presence (auric field). Here are a few preliminary steps you should take:

Perform a clearing of your mind from wandering thoughts. Focus on stillness.

Clear your emotions from any cluttered feelings.

Clear the energy of the body by bathing yourself in clean warm to hot water.

Enrobe your body and its energy field (aura) with Incense.

Next, you must take on the sensation of being aware and open.

Pause for a moment (for what feels like 1 minute) and become sensitive to all.

Let your total material form feel whatever it desires... the presence of a Tree.

Tree will let you know by sending an impulse in the form of wavy energy.

If you feel a tingling sensation around your feet or feel immersed, then contact is made and now you walk even closer to the tree without touching it. Pause every few steps, but keep moving closer to it and you should notice there is a communication through energy between yourself and the tree. Begin to employ your deep breathing more by inhaling on the tree's energy when it moves energetically toward you. As you exhale allow the energy to spread around you and back to the tree. As you keep moving toward the tree you should feel that the field of energy between yourself and the tree is stronger. Touch and embrace the tree so you can totally commune with it. Keep your own Heart's Petal of Light open as you begin to blend with it. Feel the tree's pulse through your hands, feet, entire body. Place your forehead directly on the tree and ask the Being Inside for permission to Become One with it through Unconditional Love and Harmonic Peace.

Once this very first communication is made with the tree realize it called you to it for this wonderful healing experience of Oneness. It is the pure expression of the Divine Mother coming through to accept your new found relationship. Throughout the week pay attention to what you are feeling and during the second week "see" if you have any dreams involving this energy. This "new found relationship" is really an eternal relationship that you can have with any part of the Divine Mother which has birthed us trees, mountains, water, fire, air, ores within her body and more. As you make this journey with **TREE ENERGY** via your own **BREATH** you are now beginning to realize that you are in a state of unity with Divine Mother.

Yes, this is a form of gathering because you are bringing together similar fields of energy. Once you get connected with one tree you are connected with all trees no matter where you are within the world. Remember the rings within the tree? Yes those rings represent the number of years that tree has been living...but that is living on the physical plane. You can use that same set of rings as a Symbol of Life. The Blood of the Tree is called the Sap....rearrange these letters...and sap becomes Asp which is another name for what?   Dragon, Snake and other terms. Symbolically, these two words (Dragon and Snake) also represent what is called the Cobra and movement of life force energy through your Petals of Light (that you call Chakras), vortexes and your body. As you study Tree Energy you will realize that you are relating to the vortex energies all around you and learn to be rooted. The roots of trees run deep into the earth which is to say that your roots run deep as well. You may think that your ancestral roots only pertain to your immediate family and the generations that lived before and after you on the earthly world. Your roots are connected to the celestial realm as well. Thus, Beloved Ahkenaten, Myself and so many others keep returning to remind you of these divine roots.

Let us all be seated right now…and allow yourself to connect to every part of the Divine Mother with this special invocational prayer that I will share with you all right now…gathering the forces of the Divine through this Invocational Prayer to The Divine Mother in All of Us….

Invocational Prayer to The Divine Mother

I

I call upon your Eternal Presence

&

I Seek to receive your Brilliant Light.

May you seal my wounds with your Healing Balm.

I know that you and only you shall Lift me.

So Eternal One lift me high upon your Throne.

II

O' how my Heart pines for You... The Golden One.

You are my One & Only Mother of Divine Grace.

As I exalt your name and feel you as there is no other

one but you.

We raise our Rods & Staffs to be Blessed by You.

We drink the Golden Nectar of Honey from You.

III

As I fall asleep I see the Angels within You.

I see the them as a blinding Light

and yet my eyes are well.

Despite the earth trembling beneath my feet I see the
Bold Lightning Rods
As they Dance across the Sky.
Orbs of Light of every Hue float above the Pyramids
as they Rise.
Our Pyramids disappear for a moment and then
reappear.
Diamond Flames spiral up from within them.

IV

Cobras Rising High with Emerald, Ruby and Lapis
Eyes.
Cobras dancing all around and rising out of Blue
Flames.
Blue Flames of Beloveds called I AM.
Divine Mother breathes The Holy Breath
&
I Awaken Free and Transcend as One with The Divine
Mother.

3

Your Soul's Essence is Celestial by Nature

Oh Beloveds of The Great Central Sun... You are carrying the pure essence deep within your soul. You are carrying the highest frequencies already embedded in your DNA. It is truly just a matter of activating them and reactivating others. The ones that are being reactivated are being done at a higher level. You shall be assisted by Ascended Masters and what Beloved Ahkenaten and I refer to as Transcended Masters. Transcended Masters are those who no longer have any attachments to planetary frequencies or bound to be working through them, but work with their twin flames as one flame. We can take on any form but remain on the level of walk-ins at times but we live across many "lanes" or time-lines and multi-universes simultaneously. We can function through our Pure Divine Solar Will and thus, do more than bi-locate because we have diligently with consistency and discipline have chosen to move forward without reservation. Again, I must state that no one is truly left behind unless it is by their own choice.

Many of you are beginning to grow in acute awareness and direct remembrance that you are first and foremost of the Celestial Realms. You will realize that your unique Petals of Light are interconnected to each other and the different vortexes around you. Pay more attention to your higher frequencies of the celestial nature, then you shall begin to attract and start communicating with higher beings. Many of you understand that your food intake and the types of food you consume will change. But, you must realize that your personal attitude must change as well and the way in which your "carry" yourself must change. Sometimes you have to move that miscreated ego back into place first while cleansing your aura and balancing the petals of light. You must strive to learn new skills and hone current ones.

Those who remain focused and determined to transcend themselves have done so because they keep refining their petals of light which in turn refine the different levels of awareness they can work through and continue to just upgrade. Transcenders are those who are not concerned with staying behind because there is more satisfaction when you realize that you are anchoring entire regions and planes, as well as, creating balances when necessary and stepping up your energy so that you can continue working on higher levels. You will "see and live" from higher dimensions and have the matching realms of infinite consciousness as well.

Your celestial nature is going to have you being, living as a Celestial Being souly because you simply can. Beloveds, I desire to assist you in doing this by activating you in a gentle and direct manner. But, I want you to remember this: this gentle activation is going to work through you for an indefinite period of time. Some of you are going to want to be activated through the special portals (examples: at the time of this channeled book the 11:11:11 has passed, but still the energetic frequencies are still in effect…here are a short list that comes up in 2019 as 3:3:3 and these as 3:12:30, 3:21:30, 3:30:30, 12:12:30 and 12:21:30). *You have the Transcendence Frequency as a Gateway happening in your matrix on 9: 6: 3 which is September 6th, 2019 !!!*

Beloveds, you should remember to use sound as in vocal sounds (chanting mantras and bijas), toning with tuning forks, crystal / tibetan bowls. You have colors and all kinds of symbols, gemstones and meteorites, too. Use everything you know about to help facilitate your path and for the highest good of all.

Find a quiet place where you will not be disturbed. Dim the lighting in the area you have chosen. Feel free to set the ambiance with some incense and / or candle lighting in place of overhead lighting. Allow yourself to relax through deep breathing and this in turn will help quiet your mind and calm your emotions. *It shall be much easier for you when you accept the fact that you are already that which you seek. So it is imperative that you remember that you are already a celestial being...take your time...as you first read this to see/ understand what your are going to experience....*

Close your eyes and begin to breath deeply. Allow each breath to move you deeper into your body that is increasing with an inner light...an iridescent light that is beautiful to behold...Beloveds, you notice that there is a tingling sensation happening deep within your body. You are feeling different and you have this deep desire to slightly open your eyes and notice your body is larger in stature. You feel fine and accept this reality about your body. The rhythm of your breathing has changed and you are aware that other significant changes have occurred...you feel that your joints and ligaments have stretched and you realize that things appear smaller around you. Your vision of yourself has changed and your sight is much keener than ever before...everything within your environment has shifted into a higher frequency and you realize that perhaps you truly are somewhere else but everything is now different.

The energy of this place has formed in such a way that the person and being as yourself would have to be in a body that is immense in size...and so it is and your body is both crystalline and divine for in this brief moment you begin to remember....this remembrance is happening within the library of your body, the community of your body from within the akashic element that is embedded within all of your cellular memory...this is your remembrance and it is absolutely real....it's reality first manifests within your mind - your mental body and it will take awhile for you to acclimate this feeling, but you are, as I have said before, are a celestial being by nature.

Beloveds, I know you are all wondering how can this happen, how can this really be true? What I am now revealing to you is that it is, but you merely have forgotten and that you decided eons ago to materialize in this minute form called a physical body in order to experience all things scaled down into this particular matrix. Well, there is another way and the most gentlest way and that is to DREAM THIS REMEMBRANCE FOR WHEN YOU ARE IN YOUR DREAM BODY THAT IS REAL AS WELL.

Perhaps this is a bit much for you right now, but allow me to trigger your memory -- the memory, this memory is ALREADY EMBEDDED within your cells. So, kindly remember this description of yourself...YOU ARE AN INDIVIDUAL and as an Individual you cannot divide yourself...that part that is truly yourself...your Divinely Conscious Immortal Self... ALWAYS REMAINS INTACT...the illusions split off when you reawaken to your true self. So, Beloveds you do not have to rush into doing this right now, because I desire that you meditate on this daily.

So what am I saying? What I am saying is...I AM IS STATING THIS...MY I AM PRESENCE OF THE GREAT CENTRAL SUN AS THE INFINITE IMMORTAL ONE IS ONE WITH ALL OF YOU AND NOW YOU KNOW THIS AS A REMEMBRANCE AS THE REVEALING OF THE CORRECT REALITY FOR AND IN YOU. So as I close this particular chapter allow me to leave you several seeds to help you further remember...

There can be Only One because It Is The One
That is Speaking to Itself through All of Us.
We are All One,
But, we decided to split off from The One,

And it is Now Your Time to Come Back

to Your Wealth Of Oneness within You so that You can

Activate this Reality Now.

Bring forth Your Internal State Of Your Direct

Conscious Self.

DREAM THIS REMEMBRANCE FOR WHEN
YOU ARE IN YOUR DREAM BODY THAT IS
REAL AS WELL.

4

Divine Source Code of One

Beloved Ones of The Light, this word "Code" means in so many words simply a word, text, number, symbol or image that is created to hide information to be used in secrecy....Well, there are no more secrets for everything is being revealed and everyone is a revealer of truth. Much of this releasing has to do when YOU ARE READY TO AWAKEN TO THE REALITY OF YOUR OWN DIVINITY. Every time a Soul shares his/her remembrance with you then that remembrance is an essential part that is infinite and infinitely a part of the Infinite Divine Source Code of One. So what do I mean now? The most recent channeling by Amenaten in book form entitled - "THE WISDOM OF AHKENATEN AS I AM" along with this channeling from Myself to Amenaten --- "THE GIFT - The Wisdom Of Nefertiti As I AM" is a part of the same Infinite Divine Source Code of One. *This unique paragraph is being revealed and seeded now for today is November 11, 2018 -- The Gateway of 11:11:11 right now.*

We are not the only ones teaching this as there are many more in the process of revealing and awakening within themselves. This is our goal and that is to help you awaken and remember who you have been and still are in this moment so that you can return consciously to the Oneness of The Divine Source. None of you came to just have an experience in human form and neither do you go to other realms to do only that. Many of you have returned to trigger others out of the 3D matrix so they can remember there are higher dimensions and realms of consciousness. You must remember to have FAITH for in this word is a Divine Spark called a FIAT. Fiats can be used to trigger / ignite / activate your remembrances so you can BE THE I AM.

Yes, it is difficult at times to "hold space for yourself in every moment" so you can live this awareness and remembrance as your reality. However, all of you have every thing inside of you to do it. You must consciously activate the entire process from within your Being and allow yourself to BE. You must remain centered and rooted in the revelation of your divinity and realize **you are your own master**. Beloveds, Ahkenaten and I are Masters but WE ARE NOT MASTERS OVER YOU. I repeat …. WE ARE NOT MASTERS OVER YOU. NO ONE IS HIGHER OR LOWER…to think this is an illusory thought and part of the miscreated ego.

If someone comes along and tells you that they are your master and you absorb that into your body and mind, then you become enslaved to that thought process. Then you are not free. This is called in the so-called modern world of psychotherapy "Co-dependency." Beings in the form of people trigger each other's lower-self and then they remain in the lower frequencies to battle each other and devalue each other. When people have wars they do exactly the same. That is why it is so imperative that the Souls who are awakening are to continue to do so which will bring up, amp up the divine lights throughout the surrounding environments.

The Divine Source Code of One
Means that You Are a Celestial Being known as I AM

And as a

Beloved Celestial I AM

You are Never-ending, Infinite Divine Source.

Eons ago we were always One

The word "Eons" carries within it the word

One(s)

&

We have come back again to Ascend &

Transcend.

You must remind yourself in every moment

that you shall ascend and transcend.

Every One of You carries in the cellular memory

The Divine Source Code of One!

5

God Conscious Self

Beloveds I am so happy to have come back to give this channeled spiritual transmission as my gift of wisdom to all of you. As I stated earlier, I am a God Conscious Self and that is what these words "I AM" in your language means. Kindly repeat with me now... Chant It, Sing It, Decree It:

I AM A SELF-REALIZED BEING.

I AM THAT WHICH I SAY THAT I AM.

I AM A GOD CONSCIOUS BEING

&

I DECREE THAT I COMPLETELY REMEMBER

I AM BELOVED I AM

Did you know that you have never died? Your life never ended? You could not remember that any of that happened until you decided to burst through the veils of time to consciously remember. What helps you remember is that there are many other Beings sharing this realm of conscious awareness and remembrance across all time-lines with you. You are "hearing each others thoughts" and "sensing each others feelings". These thoughts and feelings are waves traveling through the ethers and you are able to sense them during deep moments of meditation or just being in absolute silence. Remember what my Beloved Ahkenaten said:

"LET YOUR LIGHT SHINE AS I AM."
BELOVED, COME INTO THE SILENCE AND
BE LOVED!

As a God Conscious Self you are self-realized. There are infinite ways to attain this state of mind and life. You can let fear activate you, but that is not good because the energy being activated like that brings that energy into your space and it hinders everything else you strive to do. This is why you are told over and over to be careful what you think and feel and who you have around in your community of circles. Lower frequencies stagnate you and keep you immobilized. You can use happiness but that is not enough...no it is not. You must align and attune yourself to a higher frequency and ride that energy as it moves forward and especially upward.

You must use all of your available moments to reflect on your own divinity. You must realize that this is an infinite seed that is never lost. Do not let it get pressed down into you. Bring it to the surface and live it. There are millions of ways to live it. You can do lots of these:

Invoke your God Conscious Self.

Accept & Embrace this reality.

Have Faith & Trust in this Remembrance.

Affirm, Pray & Decree that You are a God Conscious Self.

Just Live as a God Conscious Self.

Do not let someone else convince you that you cannot and are not or can never be because that is their self-limiting reality.

My Beloved Ahkenaten and myself left portions of ourselves in all of our initiates and adepts as divine seeds. Now when we did that it was done with your permission and unconditional love. This means none of you are robots. You must realize   that every one awakens at their designated moment due to their own desire to move upward. We connected you to your Petals of Light through the Path of The Cobra and The Gift of The Blue Flame so that you could bring this same visionary teaching and healing to others so they can be blessed and a blessing to others in their midst. If you desire to experience the awakening of your God Conscious Self then **first use the Path of The Cobra** (Chapter 6 in The Wisdom of Ahkenaten As I AM) then refer to my wisdom key here under **"Your Soul's Essence is Celestial by Nature"** (Chapter 3) *and keep in mind that you are always the open door where silence enters and always remains.*

The Celestial Realms await for your return and in many moments these realms of divinity always arise in you. I admit this statement sounds confusing but not really. You must remember that everything and every moment is always happening inside of you including the so-called news that you hear about everyday of the earth-life. Do you know why the so-called news is real ?....It's real because you and many millions of beings in the form of people EXPECT THE NEWS TO BE REAL. This means their constant attention on it is magnetically drawing it through their emotional body. The emotional body is the magnetic side of you. You must be extra careful because as a God Conscious Self you have a very high vibrational energy field to use.

I have channeled to Amenaten earlier that the Dream World is seen as a Real Life - True Reality within itself. So with that being said the God Conscious Self can make those veils dematerialize between the dream world and the external world; the dream world will then "bleed" into the external worlds from the internal world and become the new reality. Now as you move upward with all of your Celestial essences propelling you, strive to serve by assisting others who desire to do the same by seeing what their soul signatures are and then with their permission plant the seeds of divinity within their Petals of Light (Heart, Throat, Brow, Base of Skull and Crown Centers) in their sympathetic nerve system.

As you grow in your internal awareness and remembrances you must not overlook the GCS (God Conscious Self and Essence of The Great Central Sun) in other Beings striving to do the same as you. We are all here to remind each other and to aid each other. Remember we are all one.

The Gift has arrived as I AM.
Be Love, Be Unconditional Love.
Be willing to dissolve the hatred that others
expect to be present.
Remember that Fear as Hatred carries a Lower
Frequency than Divine Love.
Beloveds You Are All I AM as well.

6

Welcome to a New Day

Beloveds, this moment right here and now is such a powerful moment. I state this because it so reminds me when we all were in the our ancient temple, and during that time Beloved Ahkenaten and I were seeing all of you graduate into the infinite higher states of consciousness through this ascension process. It was what many of you now would call a phenomenal event because we could see deeply into each one's body and see the Heart Petals of Light open up, but you had to diligently do the necessary stages to maintain your body's fields of resonance. Much courage was needed, but you did it. This was quite a feat for sure, but we could really see within your petals of light. Many of you became visionaries, healers of light, healers of sound, diviners of truth, planetary grid anchors, time travelers and many of you saw deeply into akasha with great accuracy. We knew that all of you would eventually remember how to ascend and transcend across the infinite universe.

All became adepts and all carried forth all of our teachings into the new day. Women, Men and entire families with many of the children, were adept enough with near perfect recall...your God Conscious Self revealed itself toward the end of your training. Much emphasis of the ascension training was seeded into the women first only because they carried with them the original blue print of The Divine Mother and it would be the most important training known at this time. The Divine Mother teachings were then geared to the men who in turn learned how to harness and activate along the lines and grids within in their own bodies. The children represented the Blue Diamond of Perfection, Harmony and Infinite Being with Perfect Balance. These same children would be known across many time-lines as the ones carrying what others will later call Indigo, Crystal, Rainbow with eternal youth embedded into their divine natures. This was permanently done so that the remembrance could be activated whenever and wherever the children desired to be.

I desire to bring forth a specific remembrance because as this entire insight and teachings are channeled through you it is greatly desired from the Celestials that all of you must be made aware of a program based on illusory ideas exists but only temporary. This program often referred to as "Fragmentation" and often those who think they are to enslave you desire to apply it to one's soul. This idea of fragmentation or soul fragmentation is a part of the miscreated ego program. The fragmented soul along with the miscreated ego is directly connected to separation. These programs of ill-good can be broken with the use of meditation because meditation brings you back to the center of your being and truth. So I desire to help all of you again grow this special awareness, because it is essential to being well. Read the following words as a meditation. Remember, it is important that you shield your minds and hearts from external influences.

The Soul is the Eternal Love that is Fulfilled called "Self".

The Soul is an integral vessel in which we grow with the Presence of Divinity.

The Soul represents Infinite Renewal of the Heart & Mind.

The Soul has always been known as Spirit & Star Of Universal Light.

The Higher-Self is The Soul that Sees and Knows All as One.

You are The Higher-Self and You are Ageless.

Welcome to a New Day.

7

Fear is the Opposite of Unconditional Love

The opposite of Love is Fear and hatred is the result of that fear that overwhelms one and makes that being blind with anger. Many do not know why they are so angry at all, but I can reveal to you that it all stems from self-hatred, lowering the esteem within themselves and not seeing their original value. When this happens then one can be easily influenced from external factors like others who are abusing their power and authority over another, others seeking to control others, but cannot control themselves. Those individuals lack self-esteem, dislike themselves and are often controlled by another person who lacks the same. You, as a divine being, chose to forget who you truly are in order to play "the game of life" which has been inundated with irregular changes designed to enslave your mind and disrupt the outcome of your destiny which is to return to being a Divine Being.

Sometimes it is good to keep yourself informed of what is happening around you and most of the time it is not good. The reason it is not good because what you must be made aware of is that people use the common news to infiltrate your true self with imitative thoughts designed to alter the way that you normally feel / sense, think and see life around you. These seeds are so designed to "steal away" your divinity through causing you to believe in shadow personalities. I am going to share with you a special teaching in the form of a spiritual-mental key that we gave to all of you as adepts. The key uses 4 flames embedded into your electromagnetic field as **Violet - Gold - Black - Gold**. Keep in your heart-mind that you realize that you already know. I am just helping you to remember it now. This particular key is utilized when you must detect an entity or form of energy that does not align with you on any level. It is used to identify and remove negative thought-forms and other negatives out of the electromagnetic field surrounding your physical body and physical space. The only other "tools" you will add are - a clear intention, strong will, no fear and courageous heart.

Four Raiments of Light

We are all capable and skilled to communicate with the particles of light in the ethers around us. Just focus your awareness into the energy and remember you are a spiritual sentient being. It is best to receive these as if you were putting on garments as you remember how that feels. Always keep in your mind that awareness and remembrance is how you receive more insight into what is happening around and for you. This very first raiment carries the vibration - a Violet Flame. **You must Sense, Feel in the Heart Petal of Light area or See it through the 3ʳᵈ Eye. You must use your Breath to hold and Harness.** *Let's begin right now. Place your awareness on the Heart Petal of Light and breathe in the Violet raiment and as you do Hold and Harness into the Heart Petal of Light for what feels like 30 to 60 seconds....Then, guide it through your entire internal structure (your physical body). Allow yourself to FEEL the energy (some of you might feel warm or cool tingling sensation) flow throughout your limbs and torso. Next, feel it through your pores   and guide it with your*

51

breath and mind onto your skin. Eventually, you shall feel it moving in a current within a foot or so around the body. Pause for at least 15 seconds and then with your breath and intention guide it so that it is at least arm's (including your wrist to end of fingertips) length around your body. Use more of your moments as you exhale.

*Beloveds within the next 10 seconds invoke from your Heart Petal of Light and into your 3rd Eye the second raiment carrying the **Gold Flame**. Just as you begin to Sense, Feel or See it, simply guide it into place on top of the Violet outside of your body. You should sense it and then guide another arm's length further away from your body. Hold and harness it at the Heart Petal of Light (because you will see it reflected in the 3rd Eye)...Pause again for up to 15 or 20 seconds, but remain aware for the Gold Raiment strengthens the Violet. The Violet raiment purifies you internally and externally. **It is highly important to remember that the energy as light around you is overflowing with the Spirit of Divine Intelligence. Mentally state (say): Shield & Seal** (connect your* *sense of feeling with what you are mentally saying into the electromagnetic field around you). Now, you are ready to "pull down" the third raiment carrying a* **Black Flame**. *You must extend this flame's energy twice the distance by pulling in slightly as you inhale and then while you exhale saying* **"Pah, Pah, Pah, Pah"**. *Inhale again then exhale saying* **"Pah, Pah, Pah, Pah."** *See it as Black Flames (etherically). The next step is to say: "That which does not belong here...* **in the name of The Divine I AM...Stand Up, Face Me and Get Out Now!**

Repeat the last 16 words that are underlined in bold print two more times. Then say: **"And go back from whence you came!"** *Immediately and without hesitation invoke the fourth raiment which is another* **Gold Flame** *which slightly blends into the outer edge of the Black Flame and seals it and shields everything and every part of you. The Four Raiments of Light is very powerful and real as it can be repeated whenever you desire. You do not have to wait for an emergency to occur. Beloved Ahkenaten and I desire that you use it daily to strengthen your* *electromagnetic field around your body. You can use Amethyst, Gold (metal or gem called Golden Selenite) regular Selenite and Black Tourmaline and do the same by wearing them.*

Beloveds, I am simply helping you remember what you already accomplished long ago by triggering your memory for it is within you. The use of the Four Raiments of Light will help get rid of fear and bring in more love for yourself at a high level of achievement. Also, you can do the same method using White Light.

Fear can not remain inside of you.

Dissolve the Fear.

The Beauty of Unconditional Love is in You.

You are more than enough.

You are infinite.

Everything is Internal.

Get ready to Heal and Become Whole again.

Go within and See Your Light as the Four Raiments of Light.

&

Remember You are Free !

8

The Gift of The Blue Flame

Beloveds we have arrived at another level that brings us to the Chamber within The Blue Flame. You have been gently prepared to enter into the Blue Flame which is The Divine Presence of The Great Central Sun as I AM. All of you who have been graced to be in our ancient temple will now realize that you are in essence a Temple Chamber and your Heart Petal of Light is the Aten within you.

You are the Silence within The Open Door

&

The Chamber within where Infinite Keys are

Found

But are you ready to receive your Crown?

As I say this you may feel this is a riddle to be solved. It is not because it is not a test of any kind. All of the pathways dwell deep within you and it is only when you feel that you are ready to proceed forward. There are so many ways to achieve your ascension so that you can transcend as well. When you use the Blue Flame you can stop the mind from excessively processing information or remaining too focused on the ego. As you work with the Blue Flame you will eventually develop many gifts such as: *Healing, Astromancy, Prophecy (all forms), Meditation, Soul Travel, Magnetic Healing, Crystallomancy and more.* Meditation is the root of all and so do that daily to prepare yourself so that you can delve deeper into these gifts.

This sacred flame has a Master Cell embedded into it that pulls you upward into higher realms of divinity and assists you in becoming more consciously aware of your own divinity. *This sacred flame carries the Remembrance found in Akasha that is also inside of you. Just about everything YOU have LEARNED comes FROM INSIDE OF YOU....THE REMEMBRANCE IS CONNECTED TO THE BASE OF YOUR SKULL...AKASHA IS HERE. Yes, every experience begins within you because the Soul as your Higher-Self is the Master of the journey...in fact all of your journeys. This Master Cell is a direct part of your God Conscious Self called I AM. Now you know how the Divine Source of All Sees Itself. The Gift of The Blue Flame helps you to understand this by easing and centering your mind. As the mind becomes centered and calm the Spirit of I AM can now flow down into and through all of the petals of light and grids within you.*

The Ascension Chamber

The Gift of The Blue Flame is the Gift-Key to Ascension, Transcendence and Oneness with The Great I AM in the Heart of The Great Central Sun. The Ascension Chamber is the Heart Petal of Light where you become the Blue Flame of Oneness (God Flame, Living Tree of Life, Infinite-Divine-Cosmic-Universal Mind and more).

Each adept approaches with a specific set of intentions and what one readily seeks is already within the Spirit-Mind-Heart-Body and cellular memory. All of the Divine Codes of Oneness are revealed and released from Akasha while the Adept is seated within the Ascension Chamber. When this chamber was initially setup the Adept would be there alone, but we soon realized that many needed some one to help ground them and to help record what they experienced. This was necessary because the energies within the chambers were extremely potent because of the electromagnetic frequencies embedded in them - some were in pyramids and others within the body of the Sphinx. The ones in the Sphinx were intended for at least two or more Adepts to be seated receiving healing (and learning how to soul travel) and working with the personal electromagnetic flow in their bodies. Adepts who graduated to the level of assistants were further taught how to monitor these important sessions by Ahkenaten and myself. We used a great deal of crystals and gems that were quite large. Many were positioned around the body, on the body (smaller ones) and around the chamber to help set the vibrations. We had the adepts who were made assistants "seeing the energies in stones" for healing and raising the adept's body as they sat or were laying down.

We often taught how to prepare for transition long before that moment came up in one's life. What we taught was how to Soul Travel and this was a priority. It was necessary to master the physical, emotional and mental bodies first so one had absolute control over themselves. Next, we taught all initiates how to Soul Travel. The key to all of this came through the Path of the Cobra (Chapter 6 in my Beloved Ahkenaten's book) and the other special lesson I have given you in Chapter 3 in my book. Through many days and nights we taught you all how to travel through your dreams and from your meditations. We often used sistrums and tuning forks along with our voice to subtly guide you through different worlds. But, in order to do this I must share with you a special remembrance of the Gift of The Blue Flame.

Kindly understand that these instructions were given numerous times until they were mastered by all adepts. It was very important that you remember that you are not just a spiritual sentient being, but a divine being who is 100% aware and totally conscious. You had to be able to receive, accept and embrace your divine nature as we activated it and then showed you how to protect it through the application of the Four Raiments of Light. We informed you that mushrooms such as the Reishi was designed for immortality and immortality is a real awareness and remembrance for all of us.

The Gift of The Blue Flame - Part 1 of 2

First, it is very important for our initiates to understand that all that we offered was created to act as a trigger for them to remember their own divinity and to realize they could "save others" once they saved themselves. Also, everything you learned and applied is with your own volition and at your own pace. I want to share with you exactly how Beloved Ahkenaten and I helped you have a direct experience with The Blue Flame which is the Heart of the Great Central Sun's I AM. We always guided you through the Path of The Cobra continuously to keep your energy clear so that you had control over all of your Petals of Light and the energy of the Cobra within yourself. Then, we followed that with the use of the Four Raiments of Light so that you are comfortable with its application. It is necessary to use it while in meditation, soul traveling and in your waking state as well. This way they both become a part of you. Once we sensed that you were amply prepared we proceeded with the following application.

My Beloved Ahkenaten and I raised our frequency so that we embodied the Cobraic energies. It was essential that he resonate with and radiate the Blue Cobra as it placed him in direct contact with the essence of the Divine Feminine / Divine Mother's Frequency. I already was in tune with the Divine Mother, but switched into the Golden White Flame of the Divine Masculine / Divine Father's Frequency to balance him....

My Beloved and I had this amazing connection where we could gaze into each others "eyes" and connect deeply through all of our Petals of Light to activate the Cobraic Light Energies. We often raised the energy so high that you could feel the entire area shift energetically...you could feel the electromagnetic energy move around all of us. Orbs of all kinds (colors and sacred shapes in a plasmic appearance) danced about as well. Then we would

*begin to morph and shape shift into the Living Cobras,
he changed into Blue and I turned Golden White. Our
special Gift within The Gift of the Blue Flame is that
when we became entwined as One and had raised the
energy to its highest we became the Living Gift of The
Blue Flame for at that very moment we all were in the
Heart of the Great Central Sun. This allowed the
entire place to blessed with the same and each Adept
could now pass through our Sacred flames whole and
complete. The beauty that all came to realize is that
they all had a light blue tint within their
electromagnetic field and this grew into the proper
hue every moment they experienced this special
moment. Of course, the more this was done the more
each one could then securely have their own direct
experience without our supervision. The most
important part to remember is that your
physical-emotional-mental-spiritual system along
with your nerve and sympathetic nerve systems and
petals of light MUST BE resonating on a much higher
frequency so that your body is not negatively
impacted. I emphasize this because so many from*

many civilizations and multi-universes rushed to do this without being properly grounded , centered and resonating on a correct plateau for themselves. Those individuals created illnesses, psychological and negative mental issues for themselves. Some burned themselves internally so much that burn marks showed up externally.

The Gift of The Blue Flame - Part 2 of 2

The are other means in which to accomplish this and they are very gentle procedures as well. Development through the use of Breath, Vocal Sound with Intention, Ancestors/Ancestral Guides, Angels, Crystals, Tuning Forks and more as mentioned early in this book. We have found several methods which work equally as well, but you still must diligently do your work. I shall present several more.

Pillars of the Blue Flame # 1

This method is simliar to what my Beloved Ahkenaten and I were masters at doing for the direct application for higher achievements. It takes two individual beings who are in absolute control of their own 4 part nature (physical, emotional, mental and spiritual) along with superb knowledge and voluntary control over their own Petals of Light. Both male and female is best but two males or two females works just as well. Both do the necessary breath work to expand their individual electromagnetic grids (auras). Give this at least 30 to 60 minutes individually and then do it together at the same time for at least another 30 minutes. Next, face each other and see each other as a Pillar of the Blue Flame. As this is done it is easier to raise each others frequencies without doubt. The key factor is that you can either take turns to time your breathing so that as one inhales, the other exhales. Sometimes this breathing method takes longer. So I, Nefertiti suggests that you both simultaneously inhale at the same moment and exhale at the same moment. This way you are breathing in unison as one sun. Now you both can hold and harness the Blue Flame for each other by focusing on the Heart Petals of Light, then while doing that raise upward with your focus to Throat, 3rd

Eye, Base of Skull and the Crown Petals of Light while maintaining center in the Heart Petal of Light....Pause for at least one minute to scan each other's electromagnetic fields, then signal when each are ready to focus a charge between you in the space between you (you should be at least 6 to 8 feet a part). Call forth the Blue Flame to build in the atmospheric space between the both of you...Continue to gaze into the space. Call forth the initiate to stand or sit about 3 feet from the center, then have the initiate gaze into the flame, feel it and then move their energy into the field of light. The third person can now within 5 to 10 minutes envision themselves "traveling into the portal of the Blue Flame". This entire session should be no longer than 120 minutes total from start to end. Ask the initiate to remain centered, focused and calm in order to retain what they experienced. Do this once a week until proficiency is gained and all is done smoothly.

Pillars of the Blue Flame # 2

This method works just as fine and in fact Beloved Ahkenaten and I learned this as beginners. This works when you can not find an assistant partner, then the initiate can do this alone by using two white candles and a reflective mirror. Write down your intention on parchment paper (to pass into and through the Blue Flame). If you do not have parchment paper, then use plain white paper with Black or Blue Ink. Set the candles so they are 4 feet a part. Place the mirror so that it is centered and opposite you by 3 to 6 feet away behind the candles. You are to sit facing the mirror using the same distance....Charge yourself up and Shield your electromagnetic field and entire space you choose to do this in for the moment. Make sure you are not disturbed. The only light in the area is produced by the two candles. You can also place a Blue Kyanite or White Selenite or Golden Selenite between the two candles. Draw on the candle flames as you gaze at them individually then gaze above the gemstones or paper with your intention (to experience the Blue Flame). The duration of time spent in the beginning should be approximately 30 to 45 minutes. Once a day or once per evening. Follow that regimen for at *least 9 days. Then, rest one full 24 hours, Return to doing it twice a day for 14 days to 18 days. Rest for another full 24 hours. Then practice it either morning or evening (once) daily unto you can see an image of the Blue Flame over the gems, etc. By this time you will have spent over a month without rushing the process.*

Detach from the attachment to the outcome.
You are a Being of Light and thus not ruled by man-made time.
Your Spirit and Light never expires.

Steadfast Patience along with Faith and Trust are the Keys.

9
The I AM's Solar Presence

The I AM's Solar Presence dwells in you forever even before you ever questioned if you ever had one. This is another name for "God Conscious Self, Soul, Higher-Self, Divine Presence and more. The I AM's Solar Presence dwells in the Heart of The Great Central Sun. Beloveds, you can "travel home" whenever you desire. The most popular method is to **Soul Travel**. *We are all a part of The Great Central Sun and have it's Divine Codes of Light which keeps us all intact.* This is because we have its essence within our being. You only need to have 51% overall balanced throughout the petals of light and at least have the necessary calmness and be always centered within via the **Heart Petals of Light**, and the higher petals open and clear. Here are the following steps you must use in order to insure you have a successful Soul Traveling experiences:

You must have considerable amount of experience in doing the **The Path of The Cobra** so that it literally is done with ease and at will.

You must have absolute knowledge and control to execute the **Four Raiments of Light** without doubt and no fear within you. Also, do not make a frail or fearful command. Control your emotions and thoughts well.

You should be very comfortable utilizing the **Pillar of the Blue Flame** methods (methods 1 and 2).

You should be able to successfully **Seal and Shield** your electromagnetic field immediately with one thought or two to three breaths or the basic format with ease using only **White Light** in the same manner of the Four Raiments of Light.

Always use the **Ascension Chamber** along with the **Gift of The Blue Flame** as everything that I have mentioned   is a necessity for total success. *As you use more of these last two you shall <u>begin to increase the Blue Flame within your electromagnetic energy field around your body and take on the hue of The Great Central Sun.</u>*

As we often have shared with all of our candidates, initiates and adepts - you can travel home into the Heart of The Central Sun and other destinations amongst the Celestials, as well as, communicate with them while being in true alignment and attunement with Infinite Divine Laws founded on The Laws of Absolute Unconditional Love under Divine Grace.

Beloveds, Let the Triune Laws of Divine Providence

Be as One in You.

Let Thy Sacred Spirit create sacred patterns in you as you.

The Sweetness of your Divine Wisdom is the Nectar of The One.

When you sip it, you become the Divine Remedy for All.

Embrace thy Gifts and Balance thy Ego.

We might appear to be different in appearance, but we are always One.

Separation is an Illusion.

We are The Alpha and The Omega.

We are a Never-ending Creation.

We have always been Co-Creators & Co-Partners.

We live across all time-lines and in all
multi-universes.
We are all Dancing in the Light of One Grace.
We are Ageless & Timeless.
We are Free, Eternal and always Supernal.
We are the D.N.A. ~ Divine Nature Activated.
Yes Beloveds, we are always One!

10

Pass the Torch

Usually, the passing of the torch represents the passing of one's position of   power and authority from one who has transitioned, or a soon to be retired leader to the new chosen successor. This has been a longstanding tradition in families of noble status as rulers and those belonging to religious orders. However, Beloveds will have an opportunity to continue to pass along our wisdom about the light of a new day to come that involves your light from within and the true nature of every one's divinity. This has become a very important divine mission that shall be fulfilled....

Let the I AM Presence become your glory for it is Your Infinite Truth.

It has always been every Soul's focus to return to it's divine homeland and live it's destiny as truly a Divine Being living the overflowing as its True Self in the I AM Presence within itself. We have all returned to secure this realm of thinking, being and doing this globally. This includes the emergence of the Divine Masculine Templates aligning and attuning to and with the Divine Mother's Frequency. Beloveds we shall witness the coming together, the total oneness factor as these divine truths continue to resonate with all who are ready. Those who are not quite ready will still be able to receive this like a trickle down effect and still be blessed as it triggers their own divinity as well. There are so many of you "working your divine magick" through the other layers of life from family through government plateaus. Those who still attempt to teach separation and hatred are cutting themselves off back into the illusory 3D mindset. Be aware of that, but continue to move yourselves forward so as to receive all of your blessings as they come to you now. You are all on fire from within so you must allow yourself to move forward now. As you do you shall remain in constant communication through your infinite divine nature as this is very natural. It shall always be a part of you.

The Torch within you becomes the Beacon Light for all to see.

Beloveds, you all must keep a variety of crystals and gemstones within your dwellings as they are the generators, transformers and transmitters for the selenium and other trace minerals within your current physical bodies. The use of the Selenite which was taught to you by Amenaten in Ahkenaten's book of remembrance most recently is a major key to your gift to transcend and ascend. You must remember that you have all of the four elements plus ether within your electromagnetic field. So, I choose to Pass My Torch as My Beloved Ahkenaten has done through the revelation of our remembrances and these are our divine codes of light for you to activate so that your remembrances can easily flow for you now. Keep your personal electromagnetic field clear and clean, keep it elevated.

The Divine Frequencies are real.

You are all Divine Expressions

Of

The Divine Father & The Divine Mother.

Not just One of You, but All of You.

These are principles and maxims of truth forever.

Live from your Heart Petals of Light

&

You shall see clearly that Twin Soul Flames are attracting each other.

The work - mission is going to be completed in accordance to the Divine Code of One.

I choose to speak directly with simplicity

for it triggers your awareness & remembrance.

You planted them deep within the vast layers of your consciousness.

I choose to come to you through your dreams.

The Dream World is another Reality of Remembrance.

Look for me there as it is uninterrupted and free.

Next, listen for me in your extended electromagnetic grids.

Your Altars are and can be used for Telepathic

Communication Centers.

Pyramids and Obelisks were our Communication

Generators, Transformers Transmitters & Receivers.

All of these were based on You.

Heart Petals of Light along with the others are

the generators and receivers.

Your Spine is the obelisk.

Now meditate to comprehend the rest.

Beloveds, you are the Living Standard for everything.

***Tag**, you are **T**otally **A**ctivated with **G**race.*

You are everything that you are seeking to

receive.

**So go forth and "Ceive & Receive". The Dream
World is another Reality of Remembrance. Look for
me there as it is uninterrupted and free. Next, listen
for me in your extended electromagnetic grids. Your
Altars are and can be used for Telepathic
Communication Centers.**

WE ARE ALL I AM !

11

Divine Mother's Energy

The Divine Mother's Energy emerges and impacts the core of the Divine Father by assisting all men entering with divine masculine frequencies to trust and function fully through their open Heart Petals of Light. We all are having continuous living (immortality) moments. Remember that the Divine Mother's Frequency is already intricately and infinitely a part of you by way of your cellular memory within your DNA as the D.N.A. (Divine Nature Activations) have been in motion for an eternity. *They have been coming to the surface as one evolves through one's self.* The Divine Mother's Frequency resonates with you because it is an infinite expression of your Soul's Divine Flame. Right now you are experiencing another major shift that is influencing your own emergence into the I AM Presence through the Great Central Sun...every event is occurring inside of your own electromagnetic grid along with everyone else's grid within them...this happens because of the Divine Code of One is already in motion.

We are always timeless so boundaries really overlap each other and we are not ever limited. Thus, we keep expanding our horizons by moving upward and forward. It is necessary to allow yourself to sense and feel energy that is always in motion around you, because you are a spiritual sentient being. As a spiritual sentient being you are like a star, a constellation in this world and yet you are it. *Your entire journey is to be a self-realized being and be one with all.* This is why meditation is so valuable to you. Every term that is being presented to you from Beloved Nefertiti is in essence a divine attribute. This means that you are one of the many infinite essences of Divine Mother. You are an extension and yet the pure essence of the Divine Mother is being harnessed by you as well which means you are infinite. Even though you are in a physical form, you are still expressing the divine matrix. Beloved Nefertiti says:

We have led you and shall continue to lead you back to yourself.

You are a beauty to behold and a Gift as well.

You are awakening to the truth of becoming

a Self-Realized Being.

Your are both Divine Father & Divine Mother.

You are the Divine Matrix

&

the Ultimate Expression of the Divine Code of

One.

You are all coming back home...to Your Divine

Self for an Eternity.

You are always One...One Divine Source.

Your Path is Our Path and Our Light is Your Light.

We are always evolving for we are the Open Code

&

We are Always One.

Beloveds we are raising the frequency as one electromagnetic field. We are moving and spiraling the elements within the source. The particles are breaking away from that which has never served it and you are doing the same. Therefore, Beloved Ones of The Great Central Sun you are now remembering that you are the Heart of it all. You are sovereign to and for yourself. Stay in alignment and you shall always be free. You are emerging from your cocoon like a butterfly and your wisdom is sweet like honey. You must continue on now for all to greet you and for you to embrace all that is divinely yours to behold. You are remembering to choose that you are real.

Beloveds you are remembering that YOU are an Infinite Blue Flame of the Divine Mother's energetic frequency. You are the Divine Source Code of the One Light and Law Of Unconditional Love. You are the Divine Law Of Grace and it is Your Grace that shall continue to be the Divine Intervention that shall Bless the entire Universe. Bless yourself through Her Great I AM Presence and you shall continue to be blessed in more ways than one. Unite with Her infinite flow and you shall be well.

You are an Infinite Blue Flame
of the Divine Mother's energetic frequency.
You are the Divine Source Code of the One Light
&
Law Of Unconditional Love.
You are the Divine Law Of Grace.

Beloveds, you have always been everything and you are the perpetual Divine Blue Flame. It is time for you to shine forever so that others can follow and join you now. You are like a beautiful Blue Rose. You are Abundant and Rich with Divine Love. Express yourself. Be the Logos. Be the Blue Lion. You are Free. YOU ARE THE DIVINE MOTHER'S LOVE AND CONTINUOUS LIGHT.

I

Beloveds now is your moment

to

Express the Love & Light of the Divine Mother.
You are Her Divine Agents & Now, you are The Aegis
of the Divine Mother.

II

You are the Fire of Fire. You are the Air of Air.
You are the Water of Water. You are the Earth of Earth.
You are Sacred & Divine. You are the Supernal One
to Behold. Your journey is a Brilliant Iridescent Light
for all to see.

You are Magnificent!

III

You are the Overflowing Chalice

&

Flaming Scepter.

Your Eternal Presence Blesses All.

We are in Absolute Gratitude

of

Your Divine Truth.

We Embrace & Love You for Your Light.

We Honor Your Remembrance.

We are now Whole & Complete.

12

Ahkenaten & I are One Divine Flame

My Beloved Ahkenaten & I began this journey of being Oneness eons ago by becoming later Twin Flames and despite the challenges before us, we have prevailed. We are a reflection of each other but never failed to increase our powers to see and be seen. We remained on the Path of The I AM PRESENCE with an enduring indomitable will to succeed. We came to serve all of you with the Divine Codes of Oneness. We are harbingers for each other and for all of you. Beloved Ahkenaten & I came to serve all of you with not only our stellar teaching, but with Unconditional Love, Compassion and Grace. Through the teachings of the Four Raiments of Light, the Path of The Cobra and the Gift of The Blue Flame we finally became one again. The use of mighty Selenite eased our path when it was necessary.

During our journey and life in those ancient times of Egypt, we did a great deal of Soul Traveling one at a time and then together. We did this to demonstrate before all of you how to do that and more as individuals first. Also, we did it to show you how to anchor for each other and to anchor an entire area, seal and shield it as well. We taught you that our real mission for all of us was to become a self-realized being who can consciously ascend, transcend and return to the state of oneness through the Heart of The Great Central Sun.

However, both of us had to face our fears, the fears of others and overcome them along with the miscreated ego. The most important endeavor is that we presented and taught these teachings to the non-royalty as we wanted all to know that there were no more secrets; secrecy created division and caused the miscreated ego to run rampant. Once you gain the proper control over your miscreated ego, it simply dissolves itself back into the realm of your Higher-Self (Soul). Kindly understand that all of these events did not happen immediately. There were some moments when we doubted ourselves as we dealt with the priesthood, but at some point we raised our divine frequencies enough so that no matter what they said or did, we would move forward.

My Beloved Ahkenaten says: *"Greetings Divine I AMs. Your Celestial Presence will begin to reveal itself soon enough. You must remember to develop greater self-control so you don't waste your personal energy responding to frivolous accusations, miscreated egos and pettiness that often arises as you decide to ascend. These are some of the most important occurrences that you must successfully conquer. Self-control leads to self-mastery and wellness does not happen on its own. So, you must be willing to "work on yourself" in order to achieve that state of oneness. There will always be teachers, instructors on both sides of the veil. However, if you are not willing to make an effort, then your achievements are empty and will crumble down around you. So you must remind yourself to remain centered and respond with a firm heart. What do I mean with a firm heart? I mean without any weakness or feeling helpless, because you are not helpless. Speak for yourself with courage and inner strength and you will be fine. Remember you are a spiritual sentient being and the emphasis is on spirit. You do* *not have to do everything by yourself so reach out and find your soul pods to work along with you. Often two can rise faster than one. Beyond this find and establish harmonic peace from within and love yourself unconditionally."*

Beloveds Ahkenaten and myself, Nefertiti have a blessing to give you in number 13, *but before we do that we have this meditation in words to share with you: "Clear Intention with Deep Breathing keeps you focused. Be willing to remain Aware, Rest and Rise. Stay Open to the Silence from within and you shall Rise. A Quiet Mind issues Peace, Calmness and Gentle Strength. The more you rise the greater you become. Look to develop Self-Control which leads to Self-Mastery. Even the faintest Light can be Sensed, Felt and Seen, because time is man-made and does not exist. You are actually Ageless, Timeless and Limitless. Soon you shall Remember that You have always been Self-Realized. You have always been a God Conscious Self. You are the Divine Codes of Oneness. Just like Us...You are a Divine Gift called The Celestial I AM."*

13

Beyond The Path of The Cobra

(The Gift of Soul Traveling)

Beloved Divine I AMs, before I share this additional gift with all of you for your remembrance, I must make something known to you. As we approach and pass into the new solar frequencies it is essential that you continue to enhance and raise your frequencies within your physical, emotional, mental and spiritual bodies which will influence the electromagnetic field around your bodies as well. *I suggest that during the preparation for this special gift, you should implement the Four Raiments of Light.* Take your time doing this so that you feel the field expand within itself. Also, sometimes you will see images and hear sounds which can be experienced during meditations and prayers as well. Your level of discernment will come into play the more that you use this gift. Here are a few procedures you should incorporate to insure rising success: *Energetically, clear and purify your physical space. Use Sandalwood as it calms the mind and is connected to the Great Central Sun. As you prepare your space it is good to raise the vibration within it. Clear your personal electromagnetic field as mentioned above. You can use ringing bowls or other sounds that emit peace. Connect to your ancestors and other guides if you like. Invite the assistance of a friend to help anchor the area. Use the same area of your chamber / room so that you build up its frequency. This method works best when you are not tired. Center yourself so that you are emotionally calm, mentally clear and alert.*

Practice Method #1

First, set up 2 chairs opposite each other with about 3 to 4 steps in distance from each other and sit in one of them. Next, establish your deep breathing with your personal cadence. This will keep you alert and aware. After this is done immediately use the Four Raiments of Light, then promptly "Seal and Shield" your personal electromagnetic field and the one in the chamber. Remain consciously aware of where you are in the room and what you are feeling in every moment. Next, begin to visualize seeing your etheric self seated opposite you and then with intent combined with deep breathing allow your feelings to participate. Allow yourself to feel yourself arise from one seat and walk across to the other chair and be seated. Use your inhalation to rise - stand up and walk, then exhale to be seated. Repetition is key. Allow your session to be about 20 to 30 minutes. Then, stop. You do not need to tire the mind and body, so do this daily and only once a day until you have accomplished it. Maintain a journal to chart your progress.

Practice Method # 2

Do all of the procedural steps first. Next lay down face upward on a cushioned bed. Place a cushion / pillow   under your knees, lower back and head if needed to feel more comfortable. Go into deep rhythmic breathing and remain calm and centered in the Heart Petals of Light. Expand the energy so that it is 360 degrees around your body using your intention and breath. As you continue with your breathing you shall feel your electromagnetic grid in your field expand to fill up the entire area. Continue to do this method daily and be very patient. Everyone succeeds at their own pace. Your goal is to move around the room while "out of your body". There are etheric webs or cords still connected to the physical body through your personal electromagnetic field. Maintain a journal to chart your progress.

Once you begin to get comfortable with these, then choose a familiar location outside of your dwelling such as your own yard and so forth. The more you practice the easier it becomes and you begin to grow in greater awareness and remembrance of how it feels to you. *One interesting sensation will be your back warming up, energy moving up and down the spine and along your back; another sensation is feeling both legs raise up along with the entire etheric body sliding out and above the physical. Do not consume any food until after you complete the tasks. If you decide to eat first, then wait until after an hour or more after you eat. You can drink some water before you do any of these so that you are hydrated.*

Allow yourself to review these methods by using meditation and the dream world. Remind yourself that you have successfully accomplished this with full recall (remembrance) in other lifetimes. Do this practice daily for at least 60 to 90 days. This extended method prepares you for our most important event. Remember that you are a God Conscious Self who is a Divine I AM Being and therefore a Celestial Being. Your true electromagnetic grid around your body is very large, but from inside your external form you may feel it expand as much as 10 feet in diameter. Many of you have energy fields expanding as much as 50 feet which means you can sense the area naturally. Remember I revealed to you earlier that the Dream World is a Reality more real than your physical 3D world. But, at the writing of this channeled book it is November 18, 2018 in your current life stream and you are in the midst of experiencing a shift into the 5D Matrix through Gaia with new energy flowing from the Great Central Sun through the mini-aten in your sky. The ability to soul travel is going to allow you to accomplish more in your current life stream by attracting the infinite possibilities of time lines into your current one and allow yourself to switch over into them.

Astral Traveling versus Soul Traveling

Sometimes Astral Traveling is confused with Soul Traveling. They are not the same because *astral traveling* has you venturing into lower frequencies by exploring energy fields where different entities or guardians of "lower" levels and sometimes that means where fear exists along with depressions, worry, doubt, anger and addictions, as well as, abuse dwell within the 3D matrix. Also, you can go into local areas such as where others may live (on the physical plane) but often with very little control over what you see because of its energy is not always stable. The astral plane is connected to the 3D matrix.

The Soul Plane is where the greater development of your Soul takes place with an emphasis of always being able to move forward   and you are projecting yourself into higher regions and realms where the consciousness is much higher or we say advanced. When we do this we can find ourselves having a much deeper desire to connect with those beings that are highly advanced along the upper realms. We can connect with greater ease because the realms are more stable and we have a much greater capacity to Ascend and so you will Transcend beyond and over your current environment. Thus, learning to soul travel will give you the unique level of self-mastery you originally desired so that you get past the 3D matrix and live more through the higher dimensions (5D and beyond) and be in higher "worlds" with vast consciousness in those as you are seeking to return to the Celestial.

Beloveds, you will answer the call to achieve this longing to be where the Ascended Masters, other Galactic beings and Celestials dwell as you can come back to being your original divine self. Many times your dreams have been taking you into astral realms and now there are many times when you feel and experience those realms that are vast with a much higher frequency than what you have grown accustomed to for so long. The lower petals of light keep you in line with the 3D matrix and its experiences. The Heart Petals of Light give you glimpses of the 4D where you have been able to experience Unconditional Love, rich connections to Gaia's world through the plants, animals and minerals along with the spirits of fire, air, water and earth. You learn how it is important to have the balance so you can develop greater sensitivity and respect while being humble. The application of "Tree Energy" and "Breath Work" helps you understand that everything else around you "knows, senses and feels you" and can thus communicate with you by means of telepathy.

The Gift of Soul Traveling

Beloved Ahkenaten and myself, Beloved Nefertiti desired for all of you to open up and realize that you are more than your physical form that you chose to work with and now you see its limitations. This entire channeled insight through Amenaten is being presented to you for the sole purpose of self-realization. You are celestial by nature and the way to get back into conscious awareness and to realize that you have always been communicating with the Divine Source is through Soul Travel. I have revealed to you that you must have a area where you cannot be interrupted. You can use Sound, Crystals, Incense, Oils and Candles…but these are just extensions of yourself so eventually you do not need them. There are many gemstones that are specific for this part of your journey and we have revealed that to be **SELENITE**. Selenite is known to many as a stone of flexiblity, but it carries the frequencies of INFINITE COMPASSION, UNCONDITIONAL LOVE, DIVINE GRACE AND THE DIVINE I AM. Also, it is one of the best to transmute lower frequencies into higher ones by purification.

We shall give you a "small" description of what you can discover and experience when you approach and enter into the Heart of The Great Central Sun: The Solar Flames around it are soothing. Everything comes in brighter when you GAZE RATHER THAN STARE INTO THE SCENERY. Places and Beings look larger in scale and this is true. What looks somewhat like food, air, water and more is really waves of energy. There are what we really call "Solar

Universities", "Solar Palaces", "Solar Temples" and "Solar Dwellings" in the GCS. You have to get accustomed to this so that the more you do your soul travelings the easier it becomes --- second nature becomes first nature again. Most of the time in the beginning you shall be using the Dreams and Meditations specifically set up for this major experience. You can simply reprogram yourself and the way you think and feel / sense energy so that it is easier on your physical frame. The physical frame remains behind on the physical plane and you take all of the other layers with you.You should do this with a close spiritual friend who has the same interests as you in this particular point of your life as they can monitor your body and be an anchor for you. Also, they make sure no one disturbs you sessions. You will do the same for them. What you both must understand is that your physical body will appear comatose to you. But in reality you are in the delta frequencies. The delta range is excellent for time travel into other time lines   and experiencing multi-universes as well. Once you reach a very high level of proficiency your entire area will expand...expand into miles and not feet because by that time in your experiences you will have realized that you as your soul is a celestial being that is very large naturally. Others who are not accustomed to this and still functioning from the 3D matrix will not really see you...you will appear invisible to them. You will see them along with their energy field. In fact, your energy will be high enough where they will literally walk past you and not see or hear you. They will not have a thought about entering your abode. So lets get you started with a basic way. Practice this basic way often and you shall learn very quickly.

Again, do all of the preliminary steps mentioned at the beginning. If you cannot have a close spiritual friend to assist you, don't worry just invoke your ancestors and angels to watch over you and your dwelling. Use Selenite by itself or in conjunction with these: Moldavite, Lapis Lazuli, Carnelian, Golden Selenite, Pyrite, Citrine, Tiger's Eye, Amethyst, Kyanite, Black Tourmaline and more.

*Do your meditations and request that you become aligned with a Solar Guardian. **Beloveds, Beloved Ahkenaten and I are Solar Guardians, but not the only ones.** Your etheric body will be very large so that you can have the full experience. So everything and everyone shall be "scaled up" accordingly. You must spend at least an earthly hour or so to do this. Keep in mind that "soul traveling" can feel like forever in shorter periods of time and sometimes feel short...but man-made time is suspended and therefore every moment is timeless. <u>Make sure you have plenty of rest and have allowed sufficient time to eat lightly and have digested that food well. Drink water to hydrate the physical body. You will experience a slight drop in body temperature so cover your physical body (leave the head exposed) with a light cloth-like blanket. Your heart rate and mental impulses will also slow down to coincide with delta frequencies.</u> Position your Selenite so that it is very close to your body - 3 feet or less. You can have smaller pieces in the form of grids on your body (place them on top of the covering). WE HAVE THE*

INNATE AND INFINITE CAPACITY TO BE WITH ALL OF YOU NO MATTER WHERE YOU ARE, BECAUSE WE CAN SENSE, FEEL & SEE YOU CLEARLY AS CELESTIAL BEINGS.

We are giving you a specific image so that you will have the right awareness and remembrance happening. ***The Solar Portal is The Blue Flame.*** *This flame will not harm you because it is already a part of you.* *THE BLUE FLAME IS THE FREQUENCY OF THE DIVINE MOTHER. The dwelling that you have now is turning into your personal Ascension Chamber and you are going to find your Celestial Chamber. Select to see one of your Selenites in the GCS. In essence, you shall be transporting the energy of your current chamber into the GCS. When you feel yourself in and through the blue flame just remain open in your heart and mind and you shall see and feel it there. You can hold your Selenite as a wand or rod as well. Keep your focus on the journey. The area will warm up and you will scale up to the right size. You will even experience seeing energy through walls, floors and ceilings. No matter* *what stay focused on the Blue Flame around and in the Heart of the Great Central Sun.*

How will you know if you have accomplished this? You feel overwhelmed with joy. You will feel the presence of the entire event. You will become more empathic and feel an overall sense of absolute tranquility. You will be able to actually feel and see everything. You will wonder what took you so long to have this event. You will see others that you know there as well. Your electromagnetic grid will be much larger and will cover an entire city and more if you like.

You will be able to look back into the 3D matrix and see it as a hologram. You will realize you are a Holy Gram which is a Celestial Being. Your energy and frequency will move much faster every time you return to these celestial realms and when you go back into the 3D you will not stay there and thus, will step up into the 5th Dimensional Matrix and higher ones.

You shall see all of the time-lines clearly and you shall be able to See, Feel and Sense all of the vortexes very clearly as well. You have total recall

with details of all dreams, astral and soul travelings. You shall have increased empathic, intutitive and psychic gifts. You shall have telepathic skills and many other gifts that appear otherworldly (and they are) as natural. You will be in service on a divine level.

Remember you cannot and should not rush through any of these methods for you must acclimate yourself to all of these different energetic tools. You are an energetic being that can change form, but rushing throughout without preparation will cause you to burn out and feel disjointed. You must acquire the skill to remain centered and calm. You must have control over your own mind, thoughts, feelings, body and sensations.

You are inside of an Infinite Living Vessel and every unique part of you is integral to the entire process for you are an Infinite Living Vessel as well. The more you remember, then the more you become a self-realized   Spiritual Sentient Being on a journey that is forever expanding your consciousness.

You are forever living freely as you live beyond the illusion of being separate. You are infinite so always remember:

Divine Grace is a Blessing
that belongs to All of You!

Blessings of Divine Grace
& Remembrance by Amenaten

Beloveds, I AM AMENATEN...I am one of many who have been chosen to channel this particular time-line to you for there are so many levels into infinity. These are the many "Divine Source Codes of One" that I remember. Beloved Ahkenaten and Beloved Nefertiti are always with me as they are always with you. We are all coming into the infinite folds of Divine Service to humanity and beyond. So we all shall be quite busy and yet the business of being and expressing our divinity will be one of pristine joy. Many of us will be doing more healing for ourselves, loved ones and even strangers who come into our lives. We shall have greater peace and experience extended connections with ETs and other surroundings such as Sacred Cities, Shambala, Wesak and see the crystalline grids with greater accuracy. We will have more telepathic communication and will become more of the norm which will be great so you are no longer wounded by man-made cellphone towers and underground fiber optics. You will no longer be disturbed by hidden sources designed to control your mind or body as you become immuned to them.

We are the Living Tree of Life based on a Holy Gram.

We are truly DIVINE I AMs

&

One with Divine Source.

We were once a part of the Mystery and then became a Mystic.

There is one important element for us to realize and that is that the air in the hologram is "loaded" with particles of divinity and divine light.

Yes, we are in the hologram but not of it.

We all created it along with the numerous finite roles

The awakenings will occur at a faster rate now.

You shall remember at even a much faster pace.

Beloveds Nefertiti & Ahkenaten came back to be of service in the divine ways.

Embrace their teachings as they are keys to
Self-Realization.
I Beloved Amenaten came forth to Bless you with
their teachings.

So in closing may I say this for you:

Divine Grace is Always a Blessing as it Unfolds
as a Healing Balm.
We shall continue to live in the new Age of
Remembrance.
We shall all awaken accordingly.
Many of us are Anchors for our family,
But we are Anchors for entire cities and states
And
We are never alone.
Therefore, Our Grace is Your Grace.
&
As we begin to frequently gather...

Remember that Divine Grace is a Blessing

As we are Alive & Well

In

The Age of Remembrance!

I AM BELOVED AMENATEN

About Brother Francis E. Revels-Bey

Brother Francis offers a variety of spiritual and metaphysical teachings in the form of Private and Group Classes, Seminars, Workshops, Teleseminars, YouTube Live, Facebook Live and Zoom. He is available by appointment for Spiritual Consultations by phone (and in-person if you live in Bernallilo County in New Mexico). He has been a published writer since 1981 with original articles on Numerology, Dreams, Tarot, Handwriting Analysis and Meditation. He has been a Spiritual practitioner and teacher of all of these subjects and more since 1974. He has been a guest on radio and cable tv from 1982 - 2006. He offers Spiritual Mentoring (since 1994). His current live video and radio shows are online through Blog Talk Radio and other platforms since 2008.

He arrived into this earthly world in 1952 and had his very first spiritual experience when he had what he thought at age 8 was a dream. When he told his mother, she informed him it was a vision. That vision was him attending Bard College (located in

Annandale-on-Hudson, NY). He successfully attended Bard and began having his vision unfold within the first month of his Freshman year. During his studies as an Art Major he had even more spiritual experiences and realized that his mom named Grace (who he respectfully calls Mother Grace) was his first direct spiritual teacher. He delved into the principles of yoga, meditation and martial arts in general in his Sophomore years as he was privy to work in the college used bookstore and learned the basics of Tai Chi Chuan in the beginning of his Senior year (September 1973).

He graduated from Bard College with a Bachelor's Degree in Fine Arts in June 1974 and received Honors on his Senior Project.

He has written the following books which can now be purchased on Amazon.com:

Dancing in the Light of Divine Grace
Paperback book $25.00
Kindle Ebook edition $8.88.

The Wisdom Of Ahkenaten As I AM

Paperback book $11.11

Kindle Ebook edition $7.77.

The Gift: The Wisdom Of Nefertiti As I AM

Paperback book $11.11

Kindle Ebook edition $7.77.

His future books which he is already working on are entitled: **"The Age of Remembrance"** and **"Decree & It Shall Be"**. They have their ISBNs as well.

You can reach Brother Francis E. Revels-Bey at the following emails for updates...
iam.circleofgrace1@gmail.com
iam.circleofgrace1@yahoo.com .

His current websites are:
http://CircleofGrace1.byregion.net,
https://www.youtube.com/user/CircleofGrace1,
https://Twitter.com/CirofGrace1Inst
https://www.facebook.com/CircleofGrace1

Additional Contact Information

Call his Skype Number **(505) 349-4722** ....Mondays through Fridays from 9am MST to 8pm MST (weekends vary).

You can write him at the following current mailing address below:

> **Francis E. Revels-Bey**
> **Circle Of Grace 1**
> **6100 4th Street NW #341**
> **Albuquerque, NM 87107**

Made in the USA
Las Vegas, NV
25 May 2023

72521380R00069